Giraffes
For Kids

Amazing Animal Books
For Young Readers

By Valeria Arcas
Mendon Cottage Books

JD-Biz Publishing

Read More Amazing Animal Books

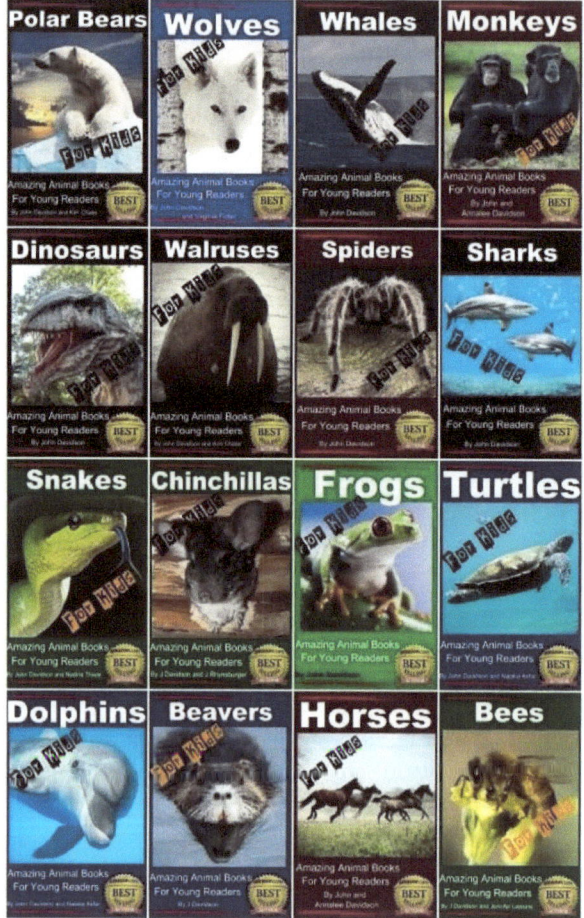

Purchase at Amazon.com

Download Free Books!
http://MendonCottageBooks.com

Table of Contents

Introduction   4

Let's Learn About Giraffes (Features)   6

Giraffes and Their Home (Habitat)   9

Chewing All Day Long. What Giraffes Eat?   11

Are You Thirsty? How Giraffes Drink?   13

Nap Time! How Giraffes Sleep?   15

The Nursery - Giraffes and Their Babies   17

Let's Talk. How Giraffes Communicate?   20

We Look the Same, But We are Not (Sub-species)   22

Please Take Care of Me   24

Come To Visit Me (Captivity)   26

A Little Bit of Information - Interesting Facts   28

Conclusion   30

Author Bio   31

Publisher   38

Introduction

Let me introduce you to one of the most beautiful and elegant animals in the African savanna, they are majestic in appearance, with an unusual body form and a peculiar gait, walking with pride, monumental in height and so peaceful, its golden spotted pattern skin shines as the sun in the savanna. The Giraffe!

You may have seen them at the zoo, as a tall plush toy in a toyshop or maybe in a movie or cartoon. These adorable creatures have a tender look that makes people want to hug and nurture them.

Together we will discover amazing facts about giraffes. Where they live and how they live? What do they eat? How they sleep? Which animals are their fiercest predators and many other interesting facts about them, come on, take your water bottle put on your explorer hat and boots (don't forget sun block too) and join me in this fantastic journey through the African savanna. Are you ready? Let's begin and enjoy your reading!

Let's Learn About Giraffes (Features)

We know them as giraffes but like all species in the world they have a scientific name, it is Giraffa Camelopardalis, it sounds a little funny right? Maybe it is better to continue naming them just "giraffe".

Giraffes are the tallest mammals on Earth; their legs are taller than many humans, 6 feet (1.80 meters) Can you believe that? Have you ever stood next to a giraffe? Probably, we would look like an ant standing next to a plant.

When giraffes are born their height is 6 feet (1.80 meters) this means a baby giraffe reaches mommy's leg. When adult females are about 16 feet (5 meters) and males 18 feet (6 meters). Males are always taller and heavier. Giraffes are as tall as a two story house!

A giraffe's tongue is 21 inch (53 centimeters) long, the inner part is pink color and turns blue gray at the visible part to protect it from sunburn while eating.

Their skin is covered by a beautiful spotted pattern, like human fingerprints. A giraffe's spotted coat is unique and different from any other giraffe. Some of these patterns look like oak leaves, others have a quadrangular shape, colors vary from light tan to dark brown almost black, same species but different as an individual.

They also have two small horns named ossicones that help to protect their head during a fight. Male ossicones don't have too much fur on top because they wear out in fights.

Giraffes' neck is 6 feet long (1.80 meters, yes again the same length of their legs) and weighs about 600 pounds (272 kg) it is very strong, it has seven vertebrae just like humans, only theirs are bigger!

These elegant friends also have a stiff mane along their neck (shorter than the one horses have). Giraffes' tail is the longest tail of any land mammal, 1 yard (91 centimeters) long with black hair at the end.

A giraffe weighs approximately from 1,100 to 2,800 pounds (500kg – 1500kg) that is your parents' car weight!

Giraffes and Their Home (Habitat)

If you could imagine the place where giraffes live, how would it be?
An open land maybe? Well giraffes live in Africa, eastern, northern and
southern part of the continent, mostly in the savanna. Have you heard
about the African savanna? It is the home of many animals such as
lions, crocodiles, hyenas, leopards, lots of birds and of course giraffes.
It is a very arid and dry place.

Giraffes roam through the savanna, grasslands and open woodlands
looking for food, especially trees. They walk in a very unique way
moving both legs on one side at the same time then the legs of the other
side.

They live and travel in small groups called herds. A herd can include both, males and females from all ages.

Giraffe's height is an advantage over other animals because they can look out for predators, even other species like to hang out with them because they are always alert, and giraffes know exactly when to run away!

Their fiercest predators are mostly humans (sad but its true), lions, crocodiles, leopards, and hyenas. They can defend themselves by kicking; giraffes are very strong animals and kick their opponent so hard they can kill them. Giraffes don't attack other animals only when they are in danger. Their spotted skin helps them to camouflage from predators.

Right know there are around 100,000 giraffes living in the wild. Giraffes can live 25 years while free in their natural environment.

Chewing All Day Long. What Giraffes Eat?

What is your favorite food? Giraffes have a favorite food too; do you have any idea of which one is their favorite food?

Giraffes are herbivorous; this means they don't eat meat, just plants and fruits. They walk long distances to find food, their favorite food is Acacia trees. They love these leaves, the same way humans love ice cream. They also eat mimosa leaves, wild apricot leaves, twigs and shoots.

Have you ever seen a giraffe eating at the zoo? They look so funny, chewing leaves with their open mouth, then chew it again and again, they can go all day long, this is because giraffes are ruminants like cows and camels, they have four compartments in their stomach and regurgitate food, after chewing and swallow it, an already chewed ball of leaves makes its way up to the mouth and then they will chew it again.

Giraffe's tongue is prehensile, they use it to pull leaves from trees, their saliva is sticky and protects the tongue and the muzzle from thorns, and so they can swallow them without hurting themselves. Giraffes also use the tongue to clean their face and horns from insects; it's so long that it reaches their ears!

How much food can you eat in a day? Giraffes spend most of the day and night eating and ruminating.

Giraffes eat a lot; they can eat 100 pounds (45 kg) of food in a single day. You know, they need to fill those 4 compartments in their stomach!

Are You Thirsty? How Giraffes Drink?

You can think that living in such hot and dry place will make giraffes thirsty all time, guess what? Giraffes don't drink water to often, on the contrary they drink two or three times a week, they can spend long periods of time without drinking water, just like camels, how do they do it? The answer is easy, giraffes get most of the water they need from leaves and fruits. Acacia leaves (their favorite) have a high content of water in them.

For a giraffe, drinking is such a difficult task; they have to bend with their front legs open they look so awkward. In this position they are vulnerable and easy target to predators. They go together to drink and take turns this way they protect to each other.

Because of the difficulty of this activity, giraffes get as much water as possible when drinking; they can drink 12 gallons of water at a single time.

Nap Time! How Giraffes Sleep?

How many sleep hours do you get at night? At least eight, well let me tell, you are a lucky kid!

There is a myth about giraffes not sleeping, well it is almost true, giraffes don't sleep as humans, they only sleep about 20 minutes a day! And they do it by taking 5-minute naps. Giraffes don't sleep at night because they keep aware from predators.

Another myth is that giraffes don't lay down, they do, they fold their legs and place their feet tucked under their body keeping the neck held up, although giraffes are napping, ruminating continues, they don't give their jaw a rest. Sometimes they do nap while standing up because it takes a long time for them to rise.

The Nursery - Giraffes and Their Babies

Giraffes can get pregnant anytime through out the year, so there are frequent births. The ritual begins with the male or bull looking for a female to breed (males can breed at 7 years old) with. They will walk side to side and then entwine their necks.

Female giraffes can get pregnant at 5 years old and carry the baby for 15 months (465 days approximately). They only have one calf (this is what baby giraffes are called).

Baby giraffes have an unusual birth, female giraffes give birth standing up, the calf falls to the ground from a height about 6.6 feet (1.80 meters) and hits its head, this bump makes the calf breathe and that's how its life begins out from mommy's belly. A newborn height is about 500- 600 cm and it weighs 150 pounds (70 kg). Babies grow 2 inches every day and double their height in about a year, that's what I call growing fast!

After half an hour after being born calves stand up and ten hours later they are able to run. Wow that's fast!

The father doesn't stick around so mom takes care of the baby. When the calf is born, mother and baby get isolated from the herd for about a week or two, and mother just leaves her calf for short periods of time while eating. The calf is hidden between trees; mommy feeds it and uses its long tongue to clean the baby. The mother protects the calf from predators like lions or hyenas. Mothers use their big hooves (the size of a plate) to kick predators.

When mommy giraffe and calf return to the herd all females become nannies and take care of the young ones, while some go to eat or drink the other ones take care of the babies.

Calves are playful, they like to jump around and run, but not too far. They drink milk from mother until 9 to 12 months old although babies can eat solid food at 4 months old when they start to ruminate.

Male calves leave their mothers at about 15 months old and look for other males to form a herd. Females stay with the mother until they are 18 months but they always stay close to the birthplace.

Let's Talk. How Giraffes Communicate?

Do you know what sound giraffes make? Have you ever listened to them? For many years people thought that giraffes were mute.

Now scientists have studied giraffes and their behavior and discovered that giraffes do make sound, well, not just one, giraffes communicate emitting whistles, roars, moos and hisses; it all depends on the occasion.

Mothers hiss to their babies when they are going far away from them.

When a giraffe is aware of a predator and thinks the herd is in danger, they begin to whistle and alert the other members of the herd.

But communicating it's not just about sounds (or words in humans case) it also is about physical movements.

Again, mothers push babies with their heads to make them move, moms also can stand between a calf and other giraffes to protect the baby from the bigger ones.

The term "necking" (when giraffes entwined their necks) can occur in two different occasions, first when a male and a female are mating, they tangled their necks. The other one is when two males are fighting or wrestling to establish dominance, they hit each other with their necks, remember they have very strong necks, you can hear some roars here.

Experts affirm that giraffes can communicate at an ultrasound level, this means humans cannot hear them. African tribes believe giraffes can predict natural disasters like earthquakes and alert other animals.

We Look the Same, But We are Not (Sub-species)

If we take a look at it we know it is a giraffe and they seem to all look alike, but some of them are lighter, some others are darker but in the end they are all giraffes.

Well surprising as it may seem they are not all the same, there exists 9 giraffe sub-species:

-**Reticulated giraffe.** Has large polygonal shaped spots, brown color. Lives in Kenya, Ethiopia and Somalia.

-**Angolan giraffe.** This one has very large spots and some notches. Lives in Angola and Zambia.

-**Kordofan giraffe.** Its spots are smaller and have an irregular form. It's found in western and southern Sudan as well as in Cameroon.

-**Masai giraffe.** This giraffe is the most different and unique of all giraffe species, it has a vine leaf shaped pattern (they really look like leaves!) the spots are dark brown. Masai giraffes are from southern Kenya and Tanzania.

-**Nubian giraffe.** Has squared spots of a chestnut brown color. Lives in eastern Sudan and northeast Congo.

-**Ugandan giraffe.** Its spots are deep brown color and rectangular shaped. It's found in Uganda and north central Kenya.

-**South African giraffe.** This giraffe has blotched star spots and lives in South Africa, Namibia, Botswana, Zimbabwe and Mozambique.

-**Thornicroft giraffe.** Star, leafy shaped spots. Lives in Zambia.

-**Nigerian giraffe.** The Nigerian giraffe is different color; it is pale yellowish with red spots. It is found as its name says in Nigeria.

Please Take Care of Me

Hunting and habitat loss are leading to the giraffes' extinction. They are killed for their tail alone to make good luck bracelets or thread for sewing, they are also hunted for their meat and hide (that gorgeous pattern skin).

Right now giraffes are not an endangered species but we need to be careful about giraffe conservation and try to eliminate hunters. Some people just hunt to keep them as a trophy.

Giraffes also are losing their habitat because of logging. Humans are cutting trees, trees that these animals need to survive.

What can we do? Avoid buying products made with giraffe body parts, avoid going on a safari trip to hunt animals, respect their environment, don't pollute, do not cut down trees, keep them in their natural habitat (as much as we love to see them at the zoo) and read, do some research about what else you can do.

Come To Visit Me (Captivity)

Giraffes are very popular animals at zoos around the world, everybody wants to see them even feed them. Visitors can see giraffes in open spaces that recreate their natural environment, although there are not as many trees as in their natural habitats.

Giraffe's lifespan in captivity is longer, almost 30 years; they have more opportunities to grow as adults in captivity because there are no predators to attack the young ones.

In captivity, a giraffe lies down more often, there is no immediate danger, and they seem more relaxed. It is true that giraffes living in captivity change their behavior, the way they use their tongue is an example, giraffes don't use their tongue as in wild to eat leaves from trees. Zookeepers give them some toys so they can keep that tongue busy!

Because of the lack of environment they modify their conduct, Diet is different at the zoo; giraffes are fed with alfalfa, bananas, grain crackers, apples and carrots.

Breeding programs in captivity are very important not only for giraffes, for all species and their future.

Many calves have been born in zoos around the world, and zookeepers take good care of them.

A Little Bit of Information - Interesting Facts

- Long time ago there was a belief that giraffes were a combination between a camel and a leopard, that is why their scientific name is camelopardalis.

- Male giraffes are called bulls, female giraffes are called cows.

- Giraffes have high blood pressure; this helps blood to reach the brain.

- A giraffe's heart weighs approximately 20 pounds (11kg) and pumps around 16 gallons of blood per minute. It's a long way to the brain and back!

- The darker the spots, the older the giraffe.

- Giraffes are great pollinators; they transfer pollen in their muzzle from a tree's flower to another.

- Back legs look shorter but they are exactly the same size of the front legs.

- A giraffe can run 35 miles per hour.

- The name giraffe comes from the Arab word "zarafa" that means the one who walks swiftly.

- They can see you in full color! Giraffes have excellent eyesight.

- Every step of a giraffe is 15 feet long.

Conclusion

It's time to say goodbye. We have learned many interesting facts about giraffes, now we know what they eat, how they live, how mothers take care of the youngest calves. We learned that giraffes are not the same and how to keep them safe.

Thank you for sharing this journey with me and I hope we can join together again for another great adventure.

Author Bio

Born in Mexico City, since a child I always loved English language, when college time arrived my decision was clear and I majored in English Language but I also like kids, teach and write. I have been a teacher for 20 years. The last few years I decided to write a children's book, then another one came and I'm on the road, it has been a great experience.

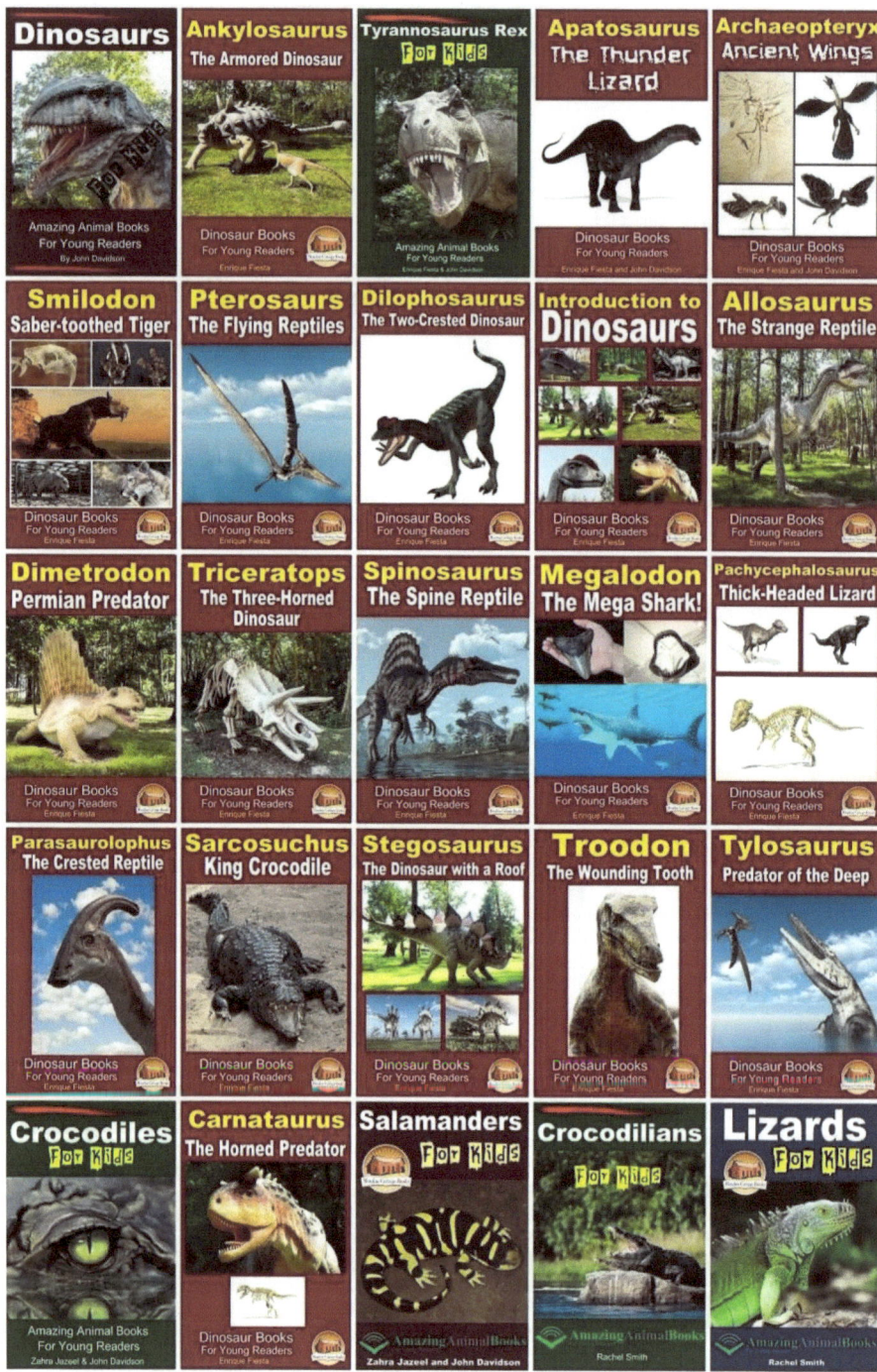

Our books are available at

1. Amazon.com

2. Barnes and Noble

3. Itunes

4. Kobo

5. Smashwords

6. Google Play Books

Download Free Books!
http://MendonCottageBooks.com

Publisher

JD-Biz Corp

P O Box 374

Mendon, Utah 84325

http://www.jd-biz.com/

www.ingramcontent.com/pod-product-compliance
Lightning Source LLC
Chambersburg PA
CBHW050856290526
45792CB00002B/609